GW00375222

DEVOTION
TO THE
SACRED HEART

All booklets are published thanks to the generous support of the members of the Catholic Truth Society

CATHOLIC TRUTH SOCIETY
PUBLISHERS TO THE HOLY SEE

CONTENTS

Acknowledgments

Prayers from the Mass of the Sacred Heart © 1974 International Committee on English in the Liturgy, Inc. All rights reserved. Psalm texts from The Jerusalem Bible, and from The Psalms, A New Translation, © 1963 The Grail (England), published by Collins in Fontana Books.

INTRODUCTION

Prayers to the Sacred Heart was first published in 1926 and revised in 1974. So well has the publication served great numbers of Catholics and, indeed, other Christian denominations in sustaining their devotion, that no modification of the original has been considered appropriate. However, some additional, introductory material has been included in the hope that it may be useful to many in their prayer and reflection.

In his encyclical, *Faith and Reason* (1998), Pope John Paul II has given us a happy and timely reminder of the efficacy and relevance of devotions which engage the mind and heart as when we consider the Heart of Our Lord, the Good Shepherd who is the Way, the Truth, and the Life. He reminds us that God, as the source of Love, "desires to make Himself known and the knowledge which the human being has of God perfects all that the human mind can know of the meaning of life." We are referred to the Second Vatican Council's Dogmatic Constitution on Divine Revelation (*Dei Verbum*): "In His goodness and wisdom, God chose to reveal Himself and to make known to us the hidden purpose of His will (cf *Ep* 1:9), by which, through Christ, the Word made flesh, man had access to the Father in the Holy Spirit and comes to share in the Divine Nature... In this revelation, the invisible God (cf *Col* 1:15; 1 *Tm* 1:17), out of the abundance of His love, speaks to men and women as friends and lives among them so that He may invite them into communion with Himself... The deepest truth about God and human salvation is made clear to us in Christ who is the Mediator and, at the same time, the fullness of all Revelation." (*Dei Verbum* 2)

"With the Incarnation of the Son of God," says the Pope, "our life is, even now, a foretaste of the fulfilment of time which is to come (cf *Heb* 1:2) and the truth about Himself and His life which God has entrusted to humanity...was declared once and for all in the mystery of Jesus of Nazareth."

No small reliance has been placed upon the Psalms, those sublime prayers that Our Lord Himself used, and the words of hymns, the beauty of which can sometimes be veiled by a concentration on the music. Devotional practices, encouraged by Mother Church as supports of faith, frequently have the benefit of 'Indulgences' attached to prayers, the words of hymns and aspirations. For that reason, a Note on Indulgences is offered as a reminder of the current teaching of the Church.

J. B. Midgley, Downham Market, November 1998

WHAT IS THE DEVOTION TO THE SACRED HEART?

History and Significance

Pope Pius XII assured us of the theological foundations of this devotion in his encyclical *Haurietis Aquas* (1956). It emanates from the most important truth of our faith: that God is present to us now in Our Lord and Saviour, true God and true Man who has ascended to dwell at His Father's right hand, His Divine Heart and the humanity He shares with us forever at one with the Blessed Trinity. Through His merits, with Him and in Him, we are the objects of a love which is continually outpoured and which is ours for the receiving. Though we cannot earn or merit God's grace or favour of ourselves, He loves us without any condition. The assurance of our justification is Our Lord's offering Himself upon the Cross as a sacrifice completely acceptable to God His Father, the shedding of His Precious Blood securing our redemption through atonement for the sin of mankind. Although we do not earn our own salvation, we can, at least, give praise to the Father for sending such a Son to deliver us. We are able to turn to the Sacred Heart and thank God even for our inadequacies and confusion and consign these to His merciful care and compassion. We seek, we find, we knock and the door is opened; we cast our care upon the Lord and our souls are rested. Although God needs neither our love nor adoration, He urges us, for our own sakes, to reciprocate His love, to open the gates of our hearts and admit the King of Glory.

Devotion to the Heart of the Word of God Incarnate focuses upon His physical heart united to His Divinity as the symbol of a redeeming and forgiving love which knows no limit. Our Lord said that living water would flow from His heart (cf *Jn* 7:37-39) and the Fathers of the Church taught that, from His pierced side, the Holy Spirit flowed upon the Church. (cf *Jn* 19:33-37)

The Middle Ages saw the recognition of the Sacred Heart as the express object of a particular and personal devotion which kept in mind the Passion and that recourse to such merciful and unbounded love prompted our emulation in respect of those who may trespass against us.

St John Eudes

John Eudes was born in Ri, Normandy, in 1601. Educated by the Society of Jesus at Caen, he was ordained a Priest of the French Oratory, Paris, in 1625 and distinguished himself as a missionary and carer of the sick during two epidemics. He founded the Institute of Our Lady of Charity, a group of Visitation Sisters, to alleviate the plight of prostitutes and, later, the Eudists, a congregation of Priests to conduct the Seminaries which he established at Caen, Coutances, Lisieux and Rouen.

He died at Caen in 1680 and was canonised in 1925. His feast day is 19th August.

He composed the Office of the Sacred Heart about 1668 and this received doctrinal and Episcopal approval in a number of dioceses. His book, *The Life and Royalty of Jesus in the Christian Soul*, promoting devotion to the Sacred Heart, had been published in 1637 but now had reached its sixth edition. The spread of the devotion is largely attributable to his pious efforts, as is the celebration of the Feast of the Heart of Our Lord in a number of Normandy Seminaries with the approval of the Bishops.

When Pope Leo XIII confirmed the heroicity of John Eudes' virtues in preparation for his canonisation, he declared him the author of the liturgical worship of the Sacred Hearts of Jesus and Mary. Pope St Pius X added that he was to be regarded as the Father of the worship of the Sacred Hearts, as the Doctor of this devotion and its apostle, for he endeavoured by his efforts to spread it everywhere.

St Margaret Mary Alacoque

Margaret Mary was born at L'Hautcour, Burgundy, in 1647. Beset as she was by delicate health, her childhood was not without its trials. At the age of twenty-four she entered the Convent of the Visitation at Paray-le-Monial and shortly afterwards, between 1673 and 1675 was favoured with visions of Our Lord who besought her to kindle devotion to His Heart as symbolising His love for mankind but which is so often rejected. Perhaps not surprisingly, her sisters in the religious life were, at first, sceptical about Margaret Mary's visions and the messages received but she received encouragement and support from a saintly Jesuit, Claude La Colombière. By the time of her early death in 1690 at the age of forty-three, community opposition had faded. Her influence on the devotional life of Catholics through her teaching and the visions she received has been great, especially since the Feast of the Sacred Heart was made general in 1856. Margaret Mary was canonised by Pope Benedict XV in 1920 and her feast day is 16th October.

"Would that I could recount," she wrote, "all that I know of the touching devotion of the Sacred Heart of Jesus and proclaim to the whole world the treasures of graces which Jesus Christ deigns to bestow in profusion on all who practice it. I know of no exercise of devotion in the spiritual life better calculated to raise a soul in a short time to the height of sanctity, and to make it taste the true sweetness which is found in the service of God. Yes, I say it with assurance, if we knew how agreeable this devotion is to Jesus Christ, there is no one Christian, how little so ever his love for this amiable Saviour, who would not practice it."

From the writings of St Margaret Mary come the twelve promises made by Our Lord to those who are devoted to His Sacred Heart:

I will give them all necessary graces for their state.
I will bring peace to their families.
I will console them in all their troubles.
I will be their assured refuge through life and
especially at death.
I will abundantly bless all their enterprises.
Sinners will find in My Heart the source and infinite
ocean of mercy.
Luke-warm souls will become fervent.
Fervent souls will rapidly advance in perfection.
I will bless the houses in which the image of My Heart
is exposed and honoured.
I will give those who work for the salvation of souls
the power of touching the most hardened hearts.
Those who propagate this devotion will have their
names inscribed on My Heart, never to be effaced.
My Heart will grant the final grace of repentance
to those who communicate on nine first Fridays
consecutively.

St Claude la Colombière

He was sent as Catholic Chaplain to the then Duchess of
York, but in 1678 was arrested on a charge of treason.
While imprisoned in London he contracted tuberculosis
and died in 1682. It is of some significance that Pope
John Paul II, canonised him in 1992 and his feast day is
15th February.

First Fridays

The devotion of receiving Holy Communion on the first Friday of each month, spending an hour each Thursday in the presence of the Blessed Sacrament and celebrating annually the Feast of the Sacred Heart.

First Saturdays

The devotion of, on five consecutive first Saturdays, receiving the Sacrament of Reconciliation, going to Holy Communion, and reciting five decades of the Rosary while meditating on its Mysteries for fifteen minutes.

Since devotion to the Sacred Heart is linked closely to veneration of the Immaculate Heart of His Blessed Mother, a consideration of the latter Feast will be found on page 59.

The Angel at Fatima

The prayer which the Angel taught the three children of Fatima:

"Most Holy Trinity, Father, Son and Holy Spirit, I adore You profoundly and offer You the most precious Body, Blood, Soul and Divinity of Jesus Christ, present in all the tabernacles of the earth, in reparation for the outrages, sacrileges and indifference with which He Himself is offended. And through the merits of His Most Sacred Heart and through the Immaculate Heart of Mary, I beg of Thee the conversion of poor sinners."

THE SOLEMNITY OF THE MOST SACRED HEART OF JESUS

Friday after the second Sunday after Pentecost

The thoughts of His heart last through every generation, that He will rescue them from death and feed them in time of famine (*Entrance Antiphon of the Feast: Psalm 32:11, 19*)

From the readings and the liturgy

Moses said to the people: 'You are a people consecrated to the Lord your God; it is you that the Lord our God has chosen to be His very own people out of all the peoples on the earth. If the Lord sets His heart on you, it was not because you outnumbered other peoples: you were the least of all peoples. It was for love of you and to keep the oath He swore to your fathers that the Lord brought you out with His mighty hand and redeemed you from the house of slavery.' (*Dt* 7:6-11)

Listen to the Word of the Lord: 'When Israel was a child I loved Him and I called my son out of Egypt. I Myself taught Ephraim to walk, I took Him in my arms; yet they have not understood that I was the one looking after them. I led them with reins of kindness, with leading strings of love. I was like someone who lifts an infant close against his cheek; stooping down to him I gave him his food.' (*Ho* 11:1, 3-4)

I myself will pasture my sheep. I myself will show them where to rest, it is the Lord who speaks. I shall look for the lost one, bring back the stray, bandage the wounded and make the weak strong. I shall watch over the fat and healthy. I shall be a true shepherd to them. (*Ezk* 34:11-16)

It is He who forgives all your guilt, who heals every one of your ills, who redeems your life from the grave, who crowns you with love and compassion. The Lord is compassion and love, slow to anger and rich in mercy. He does not treat us according to our sins nor repay us according to our faults. (*Ps* 102)

My dear people, let us love one another since love comes from God. Any one who fails to love can never have known God, because God is love. God's love for us was revealed when God sent into the world His only Son to be the sacrifice that takes our sins away... Since God has loved us so much, we too should love one another. No one has ever seen God; but as long as we love one another God will live in us and His love will be complete in us. (1 *Jn* 4:7-16)

When we were reconciled to God by the death of His Son, we were still enemies; now that we have been reconciled, surely we may count on being saved by the life of His Son? Not merely because we have been reconciled but because we are filled with joyful trust in God, through our Lord Jesus Christ, through whom we have already gained our reconciliation. (*Rm* 5:5-11)

Come to me, all of you who labour and are

overburdened, and I will give you rest. Shoulder my yoke and learn from me, for I am gentle and humble of heart, and you will find rest for your souls. Yes, my yoke is easy and my burden light. (*Mt* 11:25-30)

The soldiers came and broke the legs of the first man who had been crucified with Him and then the other. When they came to Jesus, they found He was already dead, and so instead of breaking His legs one of the soldiers pierced His side with a lance; and immediately there came out blood and water. All this happened to fulfil the words of Scripture (cf *Ex* 13:46; *Nb* 9:12; *Zc* 12:10). Not one bone of His will be broken; and again, in another place Scripture says: 'They will look on the one whom they have pierced'. (*Jn* 19:31-37)

Jesus spoke this parable to the Scribes and Pharisees: 'What man among you with a hundred sheep, losing one, would not leave the ninety-nine in the wilderness and go after the missing one till he found it? And when he found it, would he not joyfully take it on his shoulders and then, when he got home, call together his friends and neighbours? 'Rejoice with me,' he would say, 'I have found my sheep that was lost.' In the same way, I tell you, there will be more rejoicing in heaven over one repentant sinner than over ninety-nine virtuous men that have no need of repentance.' (*Lk* 15:3-7)

I am the good shepherd, says the Lord; I know my own sheep and my own know me. (Gospel Acclamation: *Jn* 10:14)

Almighty God and Father, we glory in the Sacred Heart

of Jesus, Your beloved Son, as we call to mind the great things His love has done for us. Fill us with the grace that flows in abundance from the heart of Jesus, the source of Heaven's gifts. (*Morning Prayer, Liturgy of the Hours*)

We make our prayer to Jesus in whom we find rest for our souls and who is meek and humble of heart; Jesus, your heart was pierced by the lance and from it flowed blood and water so that your bride, the Church, might be born. You were condemned by men and raised up by the Father: make the Church the tabernacle of the most high. King and centre of all hearts, in your loving mercy, you never cease to draw us to yourself: keep alive your Covenant with us all. Our peace and reconciliation, from the Cross you forgave your enemies and you bring all men together in peace. Show us how to reach the Father. Our life and resurrection, you lighten our burden and draw all sinners to yourself. Because of your infinite love, you were obedient even unto death on a cross. Bring to life all those who rest in peace. In you abides the fullness of the Godhead. Let us share in your divine nature. Beloved Lord, have mercy on us. (*Morning and Evening Intercessions, adapted, Liturgy of the Hours*)

Father, the suffering and death of your Son brought life to the whole world, moving our hearts to praise your glory. The power of the cross reveals your judgment on this world and the kingship of Christ crucified. (*From the Preface of the Passion of the Lord*)

Almighty God, the love you offer always exceeds the furthest expression of our human longing, for you are greater than the human heart. Direct each thought, each effort of our life, so that the limits of our faults and weaknesses may not obscure the vision of your glory or keep us from the peace you have promised. (*Prayer of the Church, e.g. 3rd Sunday C*)

Christ, You are the Prince of Peace,
Bid all rebellious tumults cease;
Call home Your straying sheep, and hold
Forever in one faithful fold.
For this, Your arms on Calvary
were stretched across the empurpled tree,
And the sharp spear that through You ran
Laid bare the Heart that burned for man.
(*Te saeculorum Principem, Roman Breviary*)

Jesu, grant me this I pray,
Ever in Your Heart to stay;
Let me evermore abide
hidden in Your wounded side.
Death will come one day to me;
Jesu, cast me not from Thee:
Dying, let me still abide
In Thy Heart and wounded side.
(*Dignare me, O Jesu, rogo Te*)

Almighty and Eternal God, look on the Heart of Your Beloved Son and on the praise and satisfaction He offers You in the name of sinners. Being so appeased, give pardon to all that implore Your mercy in the name of that same Son, our Lord Jesus Christ. (*Prayer concluding the Litany of the Sacred Heart*)

From the Catechism of the Catholic Church (1993)

The prayer of the Church venerates and honours the heart of Jesus just as it invokes His Most Holy Name. It adores the Incarnate Word and His Heart which, out of love for men, He allowed to be pierced for our sins. Only the Heart of Christ who knows the depths of His Father's love could reveal to us the abyss of His mercy in the beautiful parable of the Prodigal Son. (*2669; 1437*)

Once upon a time the month of June was specially devoted to the Sacred Heart and the prayers after Mass for the needs of the Church concluded, "Most Sacred Heart of Jesus, have mercy on us".

From the Psalms

In my heart of hearts, I anticipate nothing but shame and wretchedness. In vain, I looked for sympathy but there was no one to offer comfort. (*Ps* 68:21)

The Lord shows tenderness and compassion. There is no limit to His patience or His forgiveness. His anger is short-lived and He frowns only briefly. He does not treat us as our sins deserve or exact the punishment of our guilt. (*Ps* 103:8-10)

Your deeds O Lord have made me glad; for the works of Your hands I shout with joy. O Lord, how great are Your words! How deep are Your designs. (*Ps* 92:4-5)

It is he that heals the broken-hearted and binds up its wounds (Ps 146:3)

I remember the days that are past: I ponder all Your works. I muse on what Your hand has wrought and to You I stretch out my hands. Like a parched land my soul thirsts for You. (*Ps* 142:5-6)

When I see the heavens, the work of Your hands, the moon and the stars which You arranged, what is man that You should keep him in mind, mortal man that You care for him? Yet You have made him little less than a god; with glory and honour You crowned him, gave him power over the work of Your hand, put all things under his feet. (*Ps* 8:4-7)

Other readings and reflections

God's mercy is so abundant, and His love for us is so great, that while we were spiritually dead in our disobedience, He brought us to life in Christ; it is by God's grace that you have been saved. In our union with Christ Jesus, He raised us up with Him to rule with Him in the heavenly world. He did this to demonstrate for all time to come the abundant riches of His grace in the love He showed us in Christ Jesus. (*Ep* 2:4-7)

May Christ find a dwelling place, through faith, in your hearts; may your lives be rooted in love, founded on love. May you all be enabled to measure in all its breadth and length and height and depth, the love of Christ, to know what passes knowledge. (*Ep* 3:17-19)

Everyone moved by the Spirit is a son of God. The Spirit you received is not the spirit of slaves bringing fear into your lives again; it is the spirit of sons and it makes us cry out, 'Abba, Father!' The Spirit Himself and our spirit bear united witness that we are children of God. And if we are children, we are heirs as well: heirs of God and co-heirs with Christ, sharing His sufferings so as to share His glory. (*Rm* 8:14-17)

Rejoice with Jerusalem, and be glad for her, all you who love her... For thus says the Lord: 'Behold I will extend prosperity to her like a river, and the wealth of the nations like an overflowing stream; and you shall suck, you shall be carried upon her hip, and dandled upon her knees... As one whom his mother comforts, so will I comfort you; you shall be comforted Jerusalem'. (*Is* 66:10-14)

I believe that the reason behind Our Lord's great desire that especial honour should be paid to His Sacred Heart is His wish to renew in our souls the effects of our redemption. For His Sacred Heart is an inexhaustible spring which has no other purpose than to overflow into hearts which are humble so that they may be ready and willing to devote their lives to His goodwill and pleasure.

Out of this Divine Heart three streams gush forth uninterruptedly. The first stream is one of mercy for sinners to whom it brings, in its flow, the spirit of contrition and penance. The second stream is one of charity which flows to bring help to all those who are labouring under difficulties and especially to those who are aspiring after perfection, that all may find support in overcoming difficulties. But the third stream flows with love and light to those who are Christ's perfect friends, whom He wishes to bring to complete union with Himself, to share with them His own knowledge and commandments, so that they may give themselves up entirely, each in his own way, to enhancing Christ's glory. (*Office of Readings, Letters of St Margaret Mary Alacoque*)

Remember that Our Lord Jesus Christ is your true Head and you are one of His members. He is to you as the head is to members of the body; all that is His is yours. His spirit, heart, body, soul, all His faculties, all is to be used by you as if they were your own, so that serving Him you may praise Him. For your part, you are to Him as a member to the head, and He earnestly desires to use all your faculties as if they were His own for the service and glorification of His Father...

You must live by Him and for Him, and so fulfil the words of the apostle: 'None of us lives for himself and none of us dies for himself. If we live, we live for the Lord, and if we die, we die for the Lord; so then, whether we live or whether we die, we are the Lord's. For to this end, Christ died and rose again, that He might be Lord both of the dead and of the living'...

You are one with Jesus as the members are one with the head, so you must have with Him one spirit, one soul, one life, one will, one intention, one heart. It is He himself who is to be spirit, heart, love, and life, everything for you. In the life of a Christian all these marvels have their origin in Baptism, are increased and strengthened in Confirmation and the good use of the other graces in which God makes him share, and are perfected, above all, by the Holy Eucharist. (*Office of Readings, St John Eudes*)

Our Blessed Lord said: 'Whoever hears and whoever does the will of God is my brother and sister and mother'. Why brothers and sisters? Because we have a common heritage and Christ's heart of love would not be separated from us, though He is the only begotten. He will have us to be heirs of His Father and co-heirs with Himself. (*Sermon 25:7-8, St Augustine 354-430*)

In order that the Church might be formed from the side of Christ as He slept on the cross in order that the Word of Scripture might be fulfilled - 'They shall look on Him whom they have pierced' - God's providence decreed that one of the soldiers should open His sacred side with a spear so that blood with water might flow out to pay the price of our salvation. This blood which flowed out from its source, in the secret recesses of His heart, gave the sacraments of the Church power to confer the life of grace and, for those who already live in Christ, was a draught of living water welling up to eternal life. (*St Bonaventure, 1218-1297*)

Let us often prostrate ourselves before these sacred wounds, looking upon them as the source of our salvation. Let us place our hand into the wound of His side, like St Thomas, not so much to strengthen faith as to penetrate, if possible, right to the heart of Jesus, in order to draw from thence sentiments of Christian patience, entire resignation and perfect conformity to the will of God. (*Meditation for Holy Saturday, St John Baptist de la Salle, 1651-1719*)

The great and awful doctrine of the Cross of Christ, may fitly be called in the language of figure, the Heart of religion. The heart may be considered as the seat of life; it is the principle of motion, heat and activity; from it the blood goes to and from to the extreme parts of the body. It sustains the man in his powers and faculties; it enables the brain to think; and when it is touched man dies. And in like manner, the sacred doctrine of Christ's atoning sacrifice is the vital principle on which the Christian lives and without which Christianity is not. (*John Henry Newman 1801-90*)

Having given man a soul made in His own image, endowed with memory, intellect and will, and a body equipped with senses, He also created for him heaven and earth with its plenty; through love for man He created all these things, so that all these creatures should serve man, and that man, in gratitude for so many gifts, should return love for love to his Creator. (*St Alphonsus Ligouri, 1696-1787*)

THE LOVE OF GOD

He first loved us

Come to me, all you who labour and are overburdened, and I will give you rest. Shoulder my yoke and learn from me, for I am gentle and humble in heart, and you will find rest for your souls. Yes, my yoke is easy and my burden light. (*Mt* 11:28-30)

O Jesus! You are my true Friend, my only Friend. You take a part in all my misfortunes; you take them on yourself; you know how to change them into blessings. You listen to me with the greatest kindness when I relate my troubles to you, and you have always balm to pour on my wounds.

I find you at all times; I find you everywhere, you never go away; if I have to change my dwelling, I find you there wherever I go. You are never weary of listening to me, you are never tired of doing me good. I am certain of being beloved by you, if I love you; my goods are nothing to you, and by bestowing yours on me, you never grow poor; however miserable I may be, no one nobler or cleverer or even holier can come between you and me, and deprive me of your friendship; and death, which tears us away from all other friends, will unite me forever to you. All the humiliations attached to old age, or to the loss of honour will never detach you from me; on the contrary, I shall never enjoy you more fully, and you will never be closer to me than when everything seems to conspire against me to overwhelm me and to cast me down. You bear with all my faults, with extreme patience, and even my want of fidelity and my ingratitude do not wound you to such a degree as to make you unwilling to receive me back when I return to you. O Jesus, grant that I may die praising you, that I may die loving you, that I may die for the love of you. Amen. (*Saint Claude de la Colombière, d. 1682*)

Springs of living water

And you will draw water joyfully from the springs of salvation. *(Is 12:3)*

To Christ, the Prince of Peace,
and Son of God most high,
the father of the world to come,
sing we with holy joy.

Deep in his heart for us,
the wound of love he bore;
that love wherewith he still inflames
the hearts that him adore.

O Jesus, victim blest,
what else but love divine,
could thee constrain to open thus
that Sacred Heart of thine?

O fount of endless life,
O spring of water clear,
O flame celestial, cleansing all
who unto thee draw near!

Hide us in thy dear heart,
for thither do we fly;
there seek thy grace through life, in death
thine immortality.

Praise to the Father be,
and sole-begotten Son;
praise, holy Paraclete, to thee
while endless ages run.
(*German, tr. Edward Caswall, d. 1878*)

The gifts of love

Yahweh is tender and compassionate,
slow to anger, most loving;
his indignation does not last for ever,
his resentment exists a short time only;
he never treats us, never punishes us,

as our guilt and our sins deserve.
No less than the height of heaven over earth
is the greatness of his love for those who fear him;
he takes our sins farther away
than the east is from the west.
As tenderly as a father treats his children,
so Yahweh treats those who fear him.
(*from Psalm 103*)

Father, rejoice in the gifts of love
we have received from the heart of Jesus your Son.
Open our hearts to share his life
and continue to bless us with his love.
(*from the Mass of the Sacred Heart*)

Christ's promise

I will not leave you orphans; I will come back to you. In a short time the world will no longer see me; but you will see me, because I live and you will live. On that day you will understand that I am in my Father and you in me and I in you. Anybody who receives my commandments and keeps them will be one who loves me; and anybody who loves me will be loved by my Father, and I shall love him and show myself to him. (*Jn* 14:18-21)

Heart of Jesus

Heart of Jesus, you love me; grant that I may love you.
Heart of Jesus, you are always thinking of me;
grant that I may always think of you.
Heart of Jesus, you give yourself to me;
grant that I may give myself to you.
Heart of Jesus, take possession of my senses.
Heart of Jesus, take possession of my imagination.
Heart of Jesus, take possession of my memory.
Heart of Jesus, take possession of my mind.
Heart of Jesus, take possession of my will.
Heart of Jesus, grant that I may seek you
alone in all things.
Grant that I may find you in all things.
Grant that I may trust you in all things.
Grant that I may please you in all things.
Heart of Jesus, may your kingdom come
in every heart.

Be humble of heart

In your minds you must be the same as Christ Jesus. His
state was divine, yet he did not cling to his equality with
God but emptied himself to assume the condition of a
slave, and became as men are. (*Ph* 2:5-7)

Jesus, meek and humble of heart,
make our hearts like yours.

In times of discouragement

Mary went to Jesus, and as soon as she saw him she threw herself at his feet, saying, 'Lord, if you had been here, my brother would not have died'. At the sight of her tears, and those of the Jews who followed her, Jesus said in great distress, with a sigh that came straight from the heart, 'Where have you put him?' They said, 'Lord, come and see'. Jesus wept; and the Jews said, 'See how much he loved him!' But there were some who remarked, 'He opened the eyes of the blind man, could he not have prevented this man's death?' Still sighing, Jesus reached the tomb: it was a cave with a stone to close the opening. Jesus said, 'Take the stone away'. Martha said to him, 'Lord, by now he will smell; this is the fourth day'. Jesus replied, 'Have I not told you that if you believe you will see the glory of God?' So they took away the stone. Then Jesus lifted up his eyes and said: 'Father, I thank you for hearing my prayer. I knew indeed that you always hear me, but I speak for the sake of all these who stand round me, so that they may believe it was you who sent me'. When he had said this, he cried in a loud voice, 'Lazarus, here! Come out!' The dead man came out, his feet and hands bound with bands of stuff and a cloth round his face. Jesus said to them, 'Unbind him, let him go free'. (*Jn* 11:32-44)

Dear Lord, who said, 'Come to Me, all you who labour and are overburdened, and I will give you rest', behold me at your feet, O my God, burdened and suffering but full of confidence in your promise.

O my Lord and Saviour, have pity on me as you had pity on the blind to whom you gave back their sight. Have pity on me as you had pity on the deaf, whose ears you opened, and on the dumb whose tongue you loosened.

Have pity on me as you had pity on the lepers whom you made clean.

Have pity on me as you had pity on the paralysed to whom you gave back use of their limbs.

Have pity on me as you had pity on the possessed whom you saved from the power of the devil.

Have pity on me as you had pity on the young man of Naim, on Jairus' daughter, and on Lazarus whom you recalled from death to life.

Have pity on me as you had pity on the multitude whom you fed with bread in the wilderness.

Have pity on me as you had pity on the Apostles in the midst of the storm.

Have pity on me as you had pity on the Samaritan woman, and the Chanaanite.

Have pity on me as you had pity on Mary Magdalen.

Have pity on me as you had pity on the Good Thief on the Cross.

Have pity on me as you had pity on your Apostle Peter when he denied you.

O Divine Heart of Jesus, source of all resurrection, of all life, of all health, of all light, of all strength, of all consolation, of all hope, of all grace, have pity on me. (*Pere de B., SJ*)

To save, not to condemn

Yes, God loved the world so much that he gave his only Son, so that everyone who believes in him may not be lost but may have eternal life. For God sent his Son into the world not to condemn the world, but so that through him the world might be saved. (*Jn* 3:16-17)

Heart of my Creator, perfect me.
Heart of my Redeemer, answer for me.
Heart of my Father, govern me.
Heart of my Judge, pardon me.
Heart of my Advocate, plead for me.
Heart of my Master, teach me.
Heart of my Pastor, guard me.
Heart of my faithful Friend, rest in me.
Heart wounded for my love, receive me.
Sacred Heart of Jesus dying on the Cross, save me.

Fire on the earth

I have come to bring fire to the earth, and how I wish it were blazing already! (*Lk* 12:49)

Heart of Jesus, burning with love for us,
Inflame our hearts with love of You.

THE RESPONSE OF MAN

We disown Christ

Jerusalem, Jerusalem, you that kill the prophets and stone those who are sent to you! How often have I longed to gather your children, as a hen gathers her brood under her wings, and you refused! (*Lk* 13:34)

My song is love unknown,
my Saviour's love to me,
love to the loveless shown
that they might lovely be.
    O who am I,
    that for my sake
    my Lord should take
    frail flesh and die?

He came from his blest throne,
salvation to bestow;
but men made strange, and none
the longed-for Christ would know.
    But O, my Friend,
    my Friend indeed,
    who at my need
    his life did spend.

Sometimes they strew his way
and his sweet praises sing;
resounding all the day
Hosannas to their King;
    Then 'Crucify!'
    is all their breath,
    and for his death
    they thirst and cry.

They rise, and needs will have
my dear Lord made away;
a murderer they save,
the Prince of Life they slay;
    Yet cheerful he
    to suffering goes,
    that he his foes
    from thence might free.

Here might I say and sing.
No story so divine;
Never was love, dear King,
never was grief like thine!
    This is my Friend,
    in whose sweet praise
    I all my days
    could gladly spend.
(*S. Crossman, 1624-83*)

The one they have pierced

They will look on the one whom they have pierced; they will mourn for him as for an only son, and weep for him as people weep for a first-born child. (*Zc* 12:10)

> Lifted high on the cross,
> Christ gave his life for us,
> so much did he love us.
> From his wounded side flowed blood and water,
> the fountain of sacramental life in the Church.
> To his open heart the Saviour invites all men,
> to draw water in joy from the springs of salvation.
> (*from the Preface of the Mass of the Sacred Heart*)

We were still sinners

We were still helpless when at his appointed moment Christ died for sinful men. It is not easy to die even for a good man - though of course for someone really worthy, a man might be prepared to die - but what proves that God loves us is that Christ died for us while we were still sinners. (*Rm* 5:6-8)

Through the hole in his Body are opened to me, the secrets of his heart; the great pledge of his love is revealed. By these openings may I taste how sweet the Lord my God is; how sweet and mild he is, and how merciful he is to all that call upon him in truth, to all that seek him, and above all to all that love him.

I cannot be afraid of the multitude of my sins if I think of the death of my Lord, because my sins are not able to overmatch him. His nails and his spear cry to me that I am thoroughly reconciled to Christ, if I will but love him. Longinus has opened me Christ's side with his spear, and I am gone into it and there do I rest in safety. He that is afraid, let him love, for love drives out fear.

I love you, my God, I love you; and more and more would I love you. My Lord God, fairest of all the children of men, grant that I may long for you and love you as much as I would, and as much as I should. You are immeasurable and ought to be loved without measure, especially by us whom you have so loved, whom you have so saved, and for whom you have done such great and such good things. (*St Augustine, d. 430*)

The man of sorrows

Christ suffered for you and left an example for you to follow the way he took. He had not done anything wrong, and there had been no perjury in his mouth. He was insulted and did not retaliate with insults; when he was tortured he made no threats but he put his trust in the righteous judge. He was bearing our faults in his own body on the cross, so that we might die to our faults and live for holiness; through his wounds you have been healed. (1 *P* 2:21)

Give me, O divine Lord, grace so devoutly to contemplate your bitter passion, that my heart may be clothed with your bitter sufferings, and the virtue of meekness, that my sins may be covered with the purple of your tender love.

A spring of water for eternal life

Whoever drinks this water will get thirsty again; but anyone who drinks the water that I shall give will never be thirsty again: the water that I shall give will turn into a spring inside him, welling up to eternal life. (*Jn* 4:13-14)

O Jesus, my Saviour, how greatly am I indebted to you for having willed that your side should be opened with a spear, that in the depth of your Heart we might behold your great love for us, and for having permitted your Holy Body, when taken down from the Cross, to be placed in the arms of your Blessed Mother, who received it bathed in tears and with her heart broken and pierced with most bitter grief. I beseech you, O Lord, to pierce my heart with a true wound of love, to cleanse my soul from all its stains with the water that came out of your side, and to heal its infirmities with the remedy of your Blood. Grant me grace to share in the sorrows of your most holy Mother at the time of your Passion and death. Make me one of her faithful and devoted servants, that she may take me under her protection and assist me in my trials and necessities, especially at the hour of my death. (*Dom Anthony de Molina, Carthusian, c. 1605*)

He has redeemed us

Not long ago, you were foreigners and enemies, in the way that you used to think and the evil things that you did; but now he has reconciled you, by his death and in that mortal body. Now you are able to appear before him holy, pure and blameless - as long as you persevere and stand firm on the solid base of the faith. (*Col* 1:21-23)

Praise and glory be to you, most loving Jesus Christ, for the most sacred wound in your side; and by that adorable wound, and by your infinite mercy, which you made known in the opening of your breast to the soldier Longinus, and so to us all, I pray you, O most gentle Jesus, that having redeemed me by baptism from original sin, so now by your precious blood, which is offered and received throughout the world, deliver me from all evils, past, present, and to come. By your most bitter death give me a lively faith, a firm hope and a perfect charity, so that I may love you with all my heart, and all my soul, and all my strength; make me firm and steadfast in good works, and grant me perseverance in your service, so that I may be able to please you always. Amen. (*St Clare of Assisi, d. 1253*)

The Spirit will guide you

When the Spirit of truth comes he will lead you to the complete truth, since he will not be speaking as from himself but will say only what he has learnt; and he will tell you of the things to come. He will glorify me, since all he tells you will be taken from what is mine. (*Jn* 16:12-13)

Give me, O Christ Jesus, the light of your Holy Spirit to understand the value of the Cross.

O Sacred Heart, that lifted yourself up in acts of pure prayer under the stress of your agony, touch my cold heart with a spark of your fire, that I may learn to pray in the hour of sorrow and pain! O virtue of the Sacred Heart, come out and transform this heart of mine! Give me strength to grow by slow degrees more and more like you. O my Redeemer, let the hour come when there shall be nothing left in my heart or my life that I have not surrendered to you. (*Bishop Hedley, OSB., d. 1915*)

Water and the Spirit

Jesus proclaimed, 'If any man is thirsty, let him come to me! Let the man come and drink - who believes in me! As Scripture says, From his breast shall flow fountains of living water. He was speaking of the Spirit which those who believed in him were to receive. (*Jn* 7:37-39)

O God the Holy Spirit, give me sight to contemplate the love and the Passion of Jesus, that I may be changed into love and patience. Take from me selfishness, softness, self-love, delicacy, cowardice, and fear; give me a spirit of endurance, a love of labour and of the Cross, of hardness and of courage, that I may be willing to spend, and to be spent, for the elects sake. (*Cardinal Manning, d.1892*)

Reparation

Evil comes from the heart

There is no sound tree that produces rotten fruit, nor again a rotten tree that produces sound fruit. For every tree can be told by its own fruit: people do not pick figs from thorns, nor gather grapes from brambles. A good man draws what is good from the store of goodness in his heart; a bad man draws what is bad from the store of badness. For a man's words flow out of what fills his heart. (*Lk* 6:43-45)

Most Sacred Heart of Jesus, have mercy on me.
O God, forgive me for all the sins of my life:
the sins of my youth and the sins of my age,
the sins of my body and the sins of my soul,
the sins I have confessed and the sins I have forgotten,
the sins against others in thought, word and deed;
my sins of omission.
O my God, I am sorry for all my sins,
because you are so good;
and I will not sin again with the help of God.
God be merciful to me, a sinner.
Divine Heart of Jesus, convert sinners, save the dying,
deliver the holy souls in purgatory. (*Irish prayer*)

Walk in the light

This is what we have heard from him, and the message that we are announcing to you. God is light; there is no darkness in him at all. If we say that we are in union with God while we are living in darkness, we are lying because we are not living the truth. But if we live our lives in the light, as he is in the light, we are in union with one another; and the blood of Jesus, his Son, purifies us from all sin. If we say we have no sin in us, we are deceiving ourselves and refusing to admit the truth; but if we acknowledge our sins, then God who is faithful and just will forgive our sins and purify us from everything that is wrong. To say that we have never sinned is to call God a liar and to show that his word is not in us. (1 *Jn* 1:5-10)

Father, we have wounded the heart of Jesus your Son,
but he brings us forgiveness and grace.
Help us to prove our grateful love
and make amends for our sins.
(*from the Mass for the Sacred Heart*)

Change my heart

Have mercy on me, God, in your kindness.
In your compassion blot out my offence.
O wash me more and more from my guilt
and cleanse me from my sin.

My offences truly I know them;
my sin is always before me.
Against you, you alone I have sinned;
what is evil in your sight I have done.

That you may be justified when you give sentence
and be without reproach when you judge,
O see, in guilt I was born,
a sinner was I conceived.

Indeed you love truth in the heart;
then in the secret of my heart teach me wisdom.
O purify me, then I shall be clean;
O wash me, I shall be whiter than snow.

Make me hear rejoicing and gladness,
that the bones you have crushed may revive.
From my sins turn away your face
and blot out all my guilt.

A pure heart create for me, O God,
put a steadfast spirit within me.
Do not cast me away from your presence,
nor deprive me of your holy spirit.

Give me again the joy of your help;
with a spirit of fervour sustain me,
that I may teach transgressors your ways
and sinners may return to you. (*Ps 50*)

Almighty and merciful God, open my eyes to see the evil I have done. Touch my heart and convert me to yourself Where sin has separated me from you, may your love unite me to you again; where sin has brought weakness, may your power heal and strengthen; where sin has brought death, may your Spirit raise to new life. Give me a new heart to love you, so that my life may reflect the image of your Son. May the world see the glory of Christ revealed in your Church, and come to know that he is the one whom you have sent, Jesus Christ, your Son, our Lord. Amen.

Make us clean

I shall pour clean water over you and you will be cleansed; I shall cleanse you of all your defilement and all your idols. I shall give you a new heart and put a new spirit in you; I shall remove the heart of stone from your bodies and give you a heart of flesh instead. (*Ezk* 36:25-27)

God of mercy, we have sinned and our fathers have sinned before us. We have worshipped false gods, like the Israelites in the desert; we have left your house, like the prodigal son; we have nailed you to the cross, like the Roman soldiers. But you have not punished us according to our sins. Like a father, you have had compassion on us; we went our own way but you followed us. Show your love again in our days, in the Heart of your Son, which beats with mercy and compassion. Take away the

hardness of our own hearts, and make them tender and
loving like his. Fill us with the Spirit of your love who
will make us think with the mind of Christ, and bring
forth the fruits of a pure heart; and never let us forget
your mercy. Amen.

Surely they will respect my son

Jesus told the people this parable: 'A man planted a
vineyard and leased it to tenants, and went abroad for a
long while. When the time came, he sent a servant to the
tenants to get his share of the produce of the vineyard
from them. But the tenants thrashed him, and sent him
away empty handed. But he persevered and sent a second
servant; they thrashed him too and treated him shamefully
and sent him away empty handed. He still persevered and
sent a third; they wounded this one also, and threw him
out. Then the owner of the vineyard said, 'What am I to
do? I will send them my dear son. Perhaps they will
respect him.' But when the tenants saw him they put their
heads together. 'This is the heir,' they said, 'let us kill him
so that the inheritance will be ours.' So they threw him out
of the vineyard and killed him.' (*Lk* 20:9-15)

Act of reparation to the Most Sacred Heart of Jesus

Most sweet Jesus, whose overflowing charity for men is
requited by so much forgetfulness, negligence and
contempt, behold us prostrate before you, eager to repair

by a special act of homage the cruel indifference and injuries to which your loving Heart is everywhere subject.

Mindful, alas! that we ourselves have had a share in such great indignities, which we now deplore from the depths of our hearts, we humbly ask your pardon and declare our readiness to atone by voluntary expiation, not only for our own personal offences, but also for the sins of those, who, straying far from the path of salvation, refuse in their obstinate infidelity to follow you, their Shepherd and Leader, or, renouncing the promises of their baptism, have cast off the sweet yoke of your law.

We are now resolved to expiate each and every deplorable outrage committed against you; we are now determined to make amends for the manifold offences against Christian modesty in unbecoming dress and behaviour, for all the foul seductions laid to ensnare the feet of the innocent, for the frequent violations of Sundays and holydays, and the shocking blasphemies uttered against you and your Saints. We wish also to make amends for the insults to which your Vicar on earth and your priests are subjected, for the profanation, by conscious neglect or terrible acts of sacrilege, of the very Sacrament of your divine love, and lastly for the public crimes of nations who resist the rights and teaching authority of the Church which you have founded.

Would that we were able to wash away such abominations with our blood. We now offer, in reparation for these violations of your divine honour, the satisfaction you once made to your Eternal Father on the cross and which you continue to renew daily on our altars; we offer it in union with the acts of atonement of your Virgin Mother and all the Saints and of the pious faithful on earth; and we sincerely promise to make recompense, as far as we can with the help of your grace, for all neglect of your great love and for the sins we and others have committed in the past. Henceforth, we will live a life of unswerving faith, of purity of conduct, of perfect observance of the precepts of the Gospel and especially that of charity. We promise to the best of our power to prevent others from offending you and to bring as many as possible to follow you.

O loving Jesus, through the intercession of the Blessed Virgin Mother, our model in reparation, deign to receive the voluntary offering we make of this act of expiation; and by the crowning gift of perseverance keep us faithful unto death in our duty and the allegiance we owe to you, so that we may all one day come to that happy home, where with the Father and the Holy Spirit you live and reign, God, for ever and ever. Amen.

(A partial indulgence is granted to the faithful who piously recite the above act of reparation. A plenary indulgence is granted if it is publicly recited on the feast of the Most Sacred Heart of Jesus.)

You love, you are not loved

When he saw the crowds he felt sorry for them because
they were harassed and dejected, like sheep without a
shepherd. (*Mt* 9:36)

> Heart of Jesus, you love,
> you are not loved,
> O would that you were loved!
> O adorable Heart of Jesus,
> if men did but know you,
> how they would love you!
> (*Constant prayer of Père de Tournely, d. 1797*)

> Bless me, gentlest Jesus,
> bless me and have mercy on me
> according to the bounty
> of your most gentle Heart.
> (*St Gertrude*)

CONSECRATION

We will love the Lord our God

Listen, Israel: The Lord your God is the only God. You shall love the Lord your God with all your heart, with all your soul, with all your strength. Let these words I urge on you today be written on your heart. You shall repeat them to your children and say them over to them whether at rest in your house or walking abroad, at your lying down or at your rising. (*Dt* 6:4-8)

You command me to love you, O my God, who are love itself and infinitely worthy to be loved; and I wish to do so in order to respond to the very great love you have for me. But how can I love you enough? I am incapable of doing so. You are so immensely loving, and my heart is so small! I must nevertheless comply with this command given to me to love you with all my heart, with all my soul, and with all my strength. And, indeed, you have given me the means of fulfilling it through your only Son, eternal like you, and in all things equal to you. I will love you, then, O my God, through the Heart of your Son, which I possess; and as this Heart is able to love you infinitely, through it I shall love you as you deserve. (*Dom John Michael, Cathusian, d. 1600*)

I give and consecrate to the Heart of our Lord Jesus Christ, my whole life, all my actions, my trials, my sufferings, devoting every portion of my being to loving, honouring, and glorifying him, to working for his love alone, renouncing with all my heart whatever may be displeasing to him. I take you, then, O Sacred Heart, for the one object of my love, the protector of my life, the pledge of my salvation, the remedy of my inconstancy, the redeemer of all my faults, and my sure refuge in the hour of death. O Heart of all goodness, be my justification before God the Father, and shield me from the effects of his just anger. O Heart, overflowing with love, I place all my confidence in you, for I dread my own weakness, while I hope everything from your goodness. Destroy in me whatever displeases you or goes against your will. May pure love of you be so deeply imprinted in my heart that I may never forget you nor be separated from you. I implore you by all your love that my name may be graven upon you. May it be all my happiness to live and die as your slave. Amen. (*St Margaret Mary, d. 1690*)

All things in Christ

Before the world was made, he chose us, chose us in Christ, to be holy and spotless, and to live through love in his presence, determining that we should become his adopted sons, through Jesus Christ for his own kind purpose, to make us praise the glory of his grace, his free gift to us in the Beloved, in whom, through his blood, we gain our freedom, the forgiveness of our sins. Such is the richness of the grace which he has showered on us in all wisdom and insight. He has let us know the mystery of his purpose, the hidden plan he so kindly made in Christ from the beginning to act upon when the times had run their course to the end: that he would bring everything together under Christ, as head, everything in the heavens and everything on earth. (*Ep* 1:4-10)

O most sweet Jesus, Redeemer of mankind, behold us prostrate most humbly before your altar. To you we belong; yours we wish to be; and that we may be united to you more closely, we dedicate ourselves each one of us today to your most Sacred Heart.

Many have never known you; many, despising your commands, have rejected you. Have pity on them, most merciful Jesus, and draw all men to your Sacred Heart. Rule, O Lord, not only over the faithful who never have gone away from you, but also over the prodigal sons who have forsaken you; and make them return quickly to their Father's house, lest they perish of misery and hunger.

Rule over those who have been misled by error, or separated by schism; and call them back to the haven of truth and the unity of faith, so that there may soon be one fold and one Shepherd. Lastly, rule over all who are sunk in the old superstition of the Gentiles, and vouchsafe to bring them out of darkness into the light and kingdom of God.

Give to your Church, O Lord, safety and sure liberty; give to all nations peace and order; and grant that, over the whole earth, from pole to pole, may resound the words: Praise be to the Divine Heart through which was brought to us salvation; glory and honour be to it for ever. Amen. (*Pope Leo XIII, d. 1903*)

My loving Jesus! I give you my heart, and I consecrate myself wholly to you out of the grateful love I bear you, and as a reparation for all my unfaithfulness; and with your help, I propose never to sin again. Amen.

Heart of Jesus, give me only your grace and your love, and then do with me what you will. (*To be recited before the picture of the Sacred Heart*)

New life

I have been crucified with Christ, and I live now not with my own life but with the life of Christ who lives in me. The life I now live in this body I live in faith: faith in the Son of God who loved me and who sacrificed himself for my sake. (*Ga 2:20*)

Father of mercies and God of all consolation, who in your boundless love for us and your great goodness have given us the heart of your beloved Son, so that united in heart with him we may love you perfectly: grant us, we pray, that our hearts being made perfect in union with one another and with the heart of Jesus, our whole life may be a life of love between him and us, and through his mediation our lawful desires may be accomplished. (*From the Office of the Sacred Heart, composed by St John Eudes, d. 1680*)

In his footsteps

You have stripped off your old behaviour with your old self, and you have put on a new self which will progress towards true knowledge the more it is renewed in the image of its creator. (*Col* 3:9-10)

O Sacred Heart of Jesus, filled with infinite love, broken by my ingratitude, pierced by my sin, yet loving me still, accept the consecration that I make to you of all that I have and all that I am. Take every faculty of my soul and body and draw me day by day nearer and nearer to your Sacred side and there, as I may bear the lesson, teach me your blessed ways. Amen.

Strengthened with his power

We have never failed to pray for you, and what we ask God is that through perfect wisdom and spiritual understanding you should reach the fullest knowledge of his will. So you will be able to lead the kind of life which the Lord expects of you, a life acceptable to him in all its aspects; showing the results in all the good actions you do and increasing your knowledge of God. You will have in you the strength, based on his own glorious power, never to give in, but to bear anything joyfully, thanking the Father who has made it possible for you to join the saints and with them to inherit the light. Because that is what he has done: he has taken us out of the power of darkness and created a place for us in the kingdom of the Son that he loves, and in him, we gain our freedom, the forgiveness of our sins. (*Col* 1:9-14)

Since we have reached the Heart of Jesus, and it is good for us to abide in it, let us not readily turn away from it... David said: 'I have found my heart to pray to my God'. I, too, have found the Heart of the Lord my King, my Brother and my Friend, my good Jesus. And shall I not pray? Yes, I will pray. For his Heart is mine; I say it boldly. This Heart, my sweetest Jesus, which is both mine and yours I have found, and having found it, I will pray to my God... O Jesus, loveliest of all beauty, wash me more and more from my iniquity and cleanse me from my sin, that, purified by you, I may approach you, the pure One, and may be worthy to dwell in your Heart all the days of my life, that I may both see and do your will. For this cause was your side pierced that an entrance might be opened for us... Why have you been wounded again? That through the visible wound we might see the invisible wound of love... Who is there who would not love this wounded Heart? Who would not return love for love to him that has loved so well? Amen. (*St Bonaventure, d. 1274*)

O good Jesus, I praise you, adore you, and give you glory for your boundless charity, and for the tenderness of your all-loving Heart. Since from the altar of your cross you have poured out for me your precious Blood, pour out also upon me your Holy Spirit, that I may learn not to receive so great benefits in vain. Of what use would it be for me to be washed in your Blood, if I were not also enlivened by your Spirit and thus enabled to keep spotless the robes that have been washed in that Blood!

O Jesus you are loving kindness itself. From this throne of grace and pardon, the Cross, to which I see you fastened, send me your Spirit. He will teach me to give proof of my gratitude, to make my life like yours, to take part in your sufferings and death. He will show me how to return you love for love, and how to remain always faithful to you, who redeemed me at such great cost. (*Dom John of Torralba, Carthusian, d. 1578*)

The price of discipleship

If anyone wants to be a follower of mine, let him renounce himself and take up his cross and follow me. For anyone who wants to save his life will lose it; but anyone who loses his life for my sake will find it. What, then, will a man gain if he wins the whole world and ruins his life? Or what has a man to offer in exchange for his life? (*Mt* 16:24-26)

Dearest Lord, teach me to be generous, teach me to serve you as you deserve, to give and not to count the cost, to fight and not to heed the wounds, to toil and not to seek for rest, to labour and not to seek reward except that of knowing that I am doing your will.

A NEW COMMANDMENT

Love one another

This is my commandment: love one another, as I have loved you. (*Jn* 15:12)

> Father, we honour the heart of your Son
> broken by man's cruelty,
> yet symbol of love's triumph,
> pledge of all that man is called to be.
> Teach us to see Christ in the lives we touch,
> to offer him living worship
> by love-filled service to our brothers and sisters
> (*From the Mass of the Sacred Heart*)

Come into our lives

You are God's chosen race, his saints; he loves you, and you should be clothed in sincere compassion, in kindness and humility, gentleness and patience. Bear with one another; forgive each other as soon as a quarrel begins. The Lord has forgiven you; now you must do the same. Over all these clothes, to keep them together and complete them, put on love. (*Col* 3:12-14)

O Jesus, come back into our society, our family life, our souls, and reign there as our peaceful sovereign.

Enlighten with the splendour of faith and the clarity of your tender Heart, the souls of those who work for the good of the people, for your poor; impart to them your own spirit, a spirit of discipline, order and gentleness, preserving the flame of enthusiasm ever alight in their hearts. Amen. (*Prayer of Pope John*)

Fill us with your love

If I have all the eloquence of men or of angels, but speak without love, I am simply a gong booming or a cymbal clashing. If I have the gift of prophecy, understanding all the mysteries there are, and knowing everything, and if I have faith in all its fullness, to move mountains, but without love, then I am nothing at all. If I give away all that I possess, piece by piece, and if I even let them take my body to burn it, but am without love, it will do me no good whatever. (1 *Co* 13:1-3)

Lord Jesus, who walked among men, and conversing with them was found meek and humble of heart, we beseech you to increase in us those virtues which you loved so well, so that conversing among our brothers with humility and meekness, we may find rest for our souls. Amen.

Novena for the First Friday

Sacred Heart of Jesus, I unite myself:

    To your adoration,

    To your burning love,

    To your ardent zeal,

    To your reparation,

    To your thanksgiving,

    To your firm confidence,

    To your fervent prayers,

    To your silence,

    To your humility.

    To your obedience,

    To your gentleness and peace,

    To your surpassing kindness,

    To your universal charity,

    To your deep recollection,

To your intense desire for the conversion of sinners,

To your close union with the Heavenly Father,

To your intentions, desires, and will.

    Love of the Heart of Jesus,

    Inflame my heart.

    Charity of the Heart of Jesus,

    Abound in my heart.

    Strength of the Heart of Jesus,

    Uphold my heart.

    Mercy of the Heart of Jesus,

Forgive my heart.
Patience of the Heart of Jesus,
Do not weary of my heart.
Kingdom of the Heart of Jesus,
Be established in my heart.
Wisdom of the Heart of Jesus,
Teach my heart.
Will of the Heart of Jesus,
Dispose of my heart.
Zeal of the Heart of Jesus,
Consume my heart.
O Mary, conceived without sin,
pray for us to the Heart of Jesus.

Sweet Jesus, who, through your tender love for the Church your Spouse, opened to her the riches and unspeakable sweetness of your Sacred Heart, grant that our hearts may be enriched with the treasures it contains and replenished with its overflowing and unfailing delights. Amen.

DAILY PRAYERS

Prayer on awakening

I adore, praise, and salute you, O most sweet Heart of Jesus Christ. I thank you for having preserved me during this night, and for having rendered to God the Father praises and thanksgivings on my behalf. And now I offer you my heart as a morning sacrifice; I place it in your most tender Heart and entrust it to your keeping; deign to pour into it your divine inspiration, and to enkindle it with your holy love. Amen. (*St Gertrude, d. 1302*)

Morning offering

O Jesus, through the most pure heart of Mary, I offer you all the prayers, works and sufferings of this day for all the intentions of your divine Heart. O most Sacred Heart of Jesus, I place all my trust in Thee (*three times*). Amen.

For a happy death

Remember, O Lord, the word which you spoke on the cross: Father, into your hands I commend my spirit. I pray you receive my soul, when it must leave my sinful body, into the loving wound of your Heart.

O dear Lord Jesus Christ, remember how on the Cross your blessed Heart broke in the bitterness of death. When in my last hour my heart shall break in death, give me, I beseech you, this grace, that you may find in my soul perfect love, true contrition, firm faith, and unshakable trust in your mercy. Amen. (*Marienvrede, Convent of the Cross*)

Evening prayer

O good and merciful God, I thank you for keeping me this day in life and health, as also for all the good things you have given me, for body and soul, for time and eternity. I offer and commend to your holy Heart any good thing that I have by your kindness today thought, spoke, and done, and all that I have had to bear of cross and suffering.

I pray you to unite them to the love of your holy Heart, to your bitter Passion, and your merits, that they may please you and profit me to eternal life. Amen. (*From an unknown medieval author*)

A prayer for the whole world

Out of his infinite glory, may God give you the power through his Spirit for your hidden self to grow strong, so that Christ may live in your hearts through faith, and then, planted in love and built on love, you will with all the saints have strength to grasp the breadth and the length, the height and the depth; until knowing the love of Christ, which is beyond all knowledge, you are filled with the utter fullness of God. (*Ep* 3:16-19)

The Immaculate Heart of Mary

Saturday after the Second Sunday after Pentecost

Origins and Meaning

St John Eudes, 1601-80, promoted this Marian devotion in the 17th century and associated it with devotion to the Sacred Heart of Jesus. It flourished especially during the pontificates of Popes Pius VII and Pius XII who consecrated the world to the Immaculate Heart of Mary in 1942. This devotion to Mary is happily united in the Church's calendar to that of the Sacred Heart of her Son, the feast day of the one following that of the other.

Let us love and honour these two hearts which are so intimately united; let us go to God the Father through the Heart of Jesus; let us go to our Saviour through the Heart of Mary. Let us render to God the Father through the Heart of Jesus what we owe to His justice and infinite bounty, and render to God the Son through the Heart of Mary what we owe to His clemency and His benefits in our regard. We shall obtain everything from the Father and the Holy Spirit through the Heart of Jesus and everything from the Son through the Heart of Mary. (*From the Manual of Prayers, Brothers of the Christian Schools, 1952*)

Associated with this devotion is the practice of beginning each day with a prayer, the Morning Offering, by which one offers the day to God and accepts, as from the hands of God, all that comes to us in its course. The prayer relates to Our Lord's request to St Margaret Mary Alacoque and was popularised by Father Gaurelet of the Society of Jesus (1844):

"O Jesus, through the Immaculate Heart of Mary, I offer You all my prayers, works and sufferings of this day, in union with the intentions of Thy Divine Heart in the Holy Mass".

"God our Father, You created a worthy dwelling place for the Holy Spirit in the Heart of the Blessed Virgin Mary. Grant that, through her prayers, we may become a fit temple for Your glory". (*Opening Prayer of the Feast*)

From the Readings

I exult for joy in the Lord, my soul rejoices in my God, for He has clothed me in the garments of salvation, He has wrapped me in the cloak of integrity, like a bridegroom wearing his wreath, like a bridge in her jewels. (*Is* 61:9-11)

My heart exults in the Lord, I find my strength in my God... The bows of the mighty are broken but the weak are clothed with strength; it is the Lord who gives poverty and riches. He brings men low and raises them on high. He lifts up the lowly from the dust. (1 *S* 2:4-8)

(Mary and Joseph) found him in the Temple, sitting among the doctors, listening to them and asking them questions; and all those who heard Him were astonished at His intelligence and His replies. They were overcome when they saw Him, and His mother said to Him, 'My child, why have you done this to us? See how worried your father and I have been, looking for you'. 'Why were you looking for me? He replied. 'Did you not know that I must be busy with my Father's affairs?' But they did not understand what He meant. He then went down with them to Nazareth and lived under their authority. His mother stored up all these things in her heart". (*Lk* 2:46-52)

As Mary pondered all she had learned from reading and from what she had heard and seen, how greatly did she increase in faith, advance in merit and become enlightened with wisdom... In everything we do, God considers our dispositions rather than our actions. And so, whether we retire mentally to God in earnest contemplation and remain at rest or whether we are intent on being of service to those around us, let our object be that we are motivated only by the love of God. (*Sermon 8, St Laurence Justinian, 1381-1455*)

NOTE ON INDULGENCES

Several of the prayers and devotional practices set out in this booklet attract what are known as an 'indulgence', which can be of a 'partial' or 'plenary' nature.

The teachings and practice of indulgences are related to the effects of the Sacrament of Reconciliation, of our reconciliation with God and with the Communion of Saints. The doctrine is conveniently summarised in the *Catechism of the Catholic Church:*

Through indulgences the faithful can obtain remission of temporal punishment resulting from sin for themselves and also for the souls in Purgatory. (*1498*)

The Treasury of the Church is the infinite value, which can never be exhausted, which Christ's merits have before God. They were offered so that the whole of mankind could be set free from sin and attain communion with the Father. In Christ, the Redeemer Himself, the satisfaction and merits of His Redemption exist and find their efficacy. (*1476*)

This Treasury includes, as well, the prayers and good works of the Blessed Virgin Mary. They are truly immense, unfathomable and even pristine in their value before God. In the Treasury, too, are all the prayers and good works of all the saints, all those who have followed in the footsteps of Christ the Lord and, by His grace, have made their lives holy and carried out the mission the Father entrusted to them. In this way, they attained their own salvation and, at the same time, co-operated in saving their brothers and sisters in the unity of the Mystical Body. (*1477*)

The Church does not want simply to come to the aid of Christians, but also to spur them to works of devotion, penance and charity. (*1478*)

Since the faithful departed now being purified are also members of the same communion of saints, one way we can help them is to obtain indulgences for them, so that the temporal punishment due for their sins may be remitted. (*1479*)